Wild in the Strike Zone

Baseball Poems

By Tim Peeler

RANK STRANGER PRESS
MOUNT OLIVE, NORTH CAROLINA

Some of these poems have appeared in *Bold Monkey, The Dead Mule School of Southern Literature, Eclectica, EnterActive Weekly, Pudding House Publications, Spitball the Literary Baseball Magazine*, and *Tryst*.

The author wishes to thank the following people for their support: Penny Peeler, George Mitrovich, Ted Pope, Jerry Sain, David Dickson, Gary Mitchem, Mike Shannon, Betsy Teter, Diane Kistner, Cindy Coulter, Kay Gregory, Arlene Neal, Ron Rash, Tim Earley, Robert Canipe, Eric C. Harrison, Michael Loderstedt, Michel Stone, Dick Enberg, Brian McLawhorn, and Sam Silva.

Special Thanks to the great communicator, Charlie Whitley.

Cover from personal archives: 1968 Hickory Little League All-Star Team
Author Photo: Penny Abernethy Peeler

Published by
Rank Stranger Press
Mount Olive, North Carolina

ISBN-13:
978-0692719701 (Rank Stranger Press)

ISBN-10:0692719709

INTRODUCTION

I have a lot of books, more than 5,000, at last count. But if you were to ask when Tim Peeler's "Waiting for Godot's First Pitch" came into my possession, or "Touching All the Bases," I would be clueless.

But when I finally got around to reading Tim's poetry on America's Game, to actually focus on his work, I became a fan.

I was so impressed I looked him up, down there in North Carolina, and through McFarland, his publisher, was able to reach him and invite him to speak to The Writers Series I chair for the Boston Red Sox. Tim had not been to Massachusetts before, so persuading him to come was not difficult, the Red Sox being the Red Sox and all.

I am so glad he accepted my invitation and came and shared his wonderful poetry on baseball with a small group of us over lunch on a Saturday during the season (and he came in a good year, as the Sox won the American League pennant and World Series).

If I wrote that I'm a serious reader of poetry, that would be a fib; I'm not – but I am a serious reader. Books and writers fill my life, and have since my early 20s. And when you run three major public forums, The City Club of San Diego, The Denver Forum, and The Writers Series, public forums often involving writers and their works, from Peter Matthiessen to Gloria Steinem, from George Plimpton to George Will, from Jane Smiley to Richard Reeves, from Arthur Schlesinger to Peter Gay, and several hundred others, writers and their works matter – a lot.

To write books is hard. To write books that sell is problematic – very. But to write books of poetry and to think they will sell is delusional.

The millions.com web site (a happenstance finding), said this about poetry:

"Although the audience for poetry is vast, despite the very hard and creative work being done by publishers, this wider audience hasn't yet crossed the bridge from reading poetry into buying poetry books."

One half of that statement is true, about readers having yet to cross "the bridge from reading to buying." The part about "the audience for poetry is vast," is demonstrably untrue. Unless, its author believes seven billion people in the world are waiting to buy books of poetry – an idea too looney-tunes for looney-tunes.

Jeremy Spencer, writing for realpants.com in January of '15, said some books of poetry only sell 25-30 copies. The publisher of Grove/Atlantic said, according to Spencer, their sale of poetry books averages 800. A book of poetry reviewed in *The New York Times Book Review* can mean sales of 2,000-4,000 (aberrational? Yes).

But even when you weigh The Times number against 318 million of us wedged between Canada and Mexico, books of poetry have a tough go – very.

But that "tough go" is unrelated to the art of writing poetry; which is a very high art form, indeed – and one that Brother Peeler excels at.

How good is Tim?

This good:

Five days a week during the baseball season I write Baseball Notes, something I've done for four years. My readership is small (though not insignificant). I always end Notes with "Quote of the Day."

Frequently, I close Notes with one of Tim's poems on America's Game.

On one of those occasions, a regular reader of Notes, Dick Enberg, television voice of the San Diego Padres and Baseball Hall of Fame Broadcaster, was so moved by a Peeler poem he called me to say he was putting it in a special folder with instructions for it to be read at his memorial service.

Talk about the power of poetry; what greater tribute could be paid to the Bard of the Carolinas, Tim Peeler, than to have the greatest sports broadcasters ever, Dick Enberg, say the last thing he wants family, friends and admirers to remember about him is he loved the poetry of Tim Peeler.

Oh, my!

George Mitrovich
Chair, Great Fenway Park Writers Series

NOTE FROM THE AUTHOR

I was born in Reidsville, NC, but spent my childhood in Hickory, NC. My dad was a Lutheran minister who was raised in rural Rowan County and loved baseball but had no one to play with growing up. He instilled a love for the game in my brother and me at an early age. We both played into our high school years. I probably played too much too early because I gave it up for track my last two years of high school. But I never lost my love for the game, and after college when I began writing, I discovered a literary magazine called SPITBALL in Cincinnati that published all baseball-related literature. I started sending them poems about baseball in the early 80s and eventually published two full-length books of baseball themed poetry: *Touching All the Bases* and *Waiting for Godot's First Pitch*.

Since then, I have written 12 other books including four on local or regional baseball history. Two are on baseball in Catawba County, one is about the depression era outlaw Carolina League in the Piedmont of NC, and the last one is about the Easter Monday baseball game between North Carolina State and Wake Forest University.

The poems collected in *Wild in the Strike Zone* are gleaned from my work over the past fifteen years. They revisit many of the themes from my earlier work but also include sections on minor league players and outlaw baseball legends. This book is dedicated to R.G. "Hank" Utley who went to the field of dreams two years ago. Mr. Utley was a ball player and passionate historian who introduced me to the "outlaw lore." *Wild* also contains several poems based on the memories of my longtime colleague and tennis partner, John Billy Baird, who left us in 2014.

My fascination for the game continues. Even as I compose these notes and finalize this manuscript, I am writing more poems from baseball, and so I will finish this with one:

DNA 5

We were barefoot, bee stung, shirtless,
Riding bikes on washboard dirt roads,
Carrying ball gloves, a bat strapped
Across the handlebars, Momma
Calling us home for dinner from
The parsonage porch on the hill
As Dad's church chimed "Rock of Ages,"
And we raced the last steps to see
Who'd get to select the TV
Station—there were only two
Of them, and only two of us.

Tim Peeler
August 2016

TABLE OF CONTENTS

Chapter Two—Outlaws

x

In Memory of R. G. "Hank" Utley

1. WILD IN THE STRIKE ZONE

WILD IN THE STRIKE ZONE, 1965

He was thirty-nine in '65, carting us around
In a Nash four door because it made sense
When you were picking up kids for church
And picking up kids for games and taking
Kids home from school; it made sense
For a preacher and a teacher salary
To drive cheap cars that I never remember
Breaking down on the side of the road
With a bat bag in the trunk or a sermon
With the first line in each paragraph
Typed in red CAPITALS on an ancient Royal
Tucked in his jacket pocket like a passport
That he believed could win this game.

BASEBALL AND JAZZ

Cousins on this continent
risen in prisons and fields.

One caught the sun in its palm;
the other fluttered like a

moth at a gas lamp, airborne,
playing as if to stop would

crash; knuckle balls and slow curves
as the wino shies from the

fire barrel in the alley
after the elastic flight

of the day took him to the
dumpster by the stadium

where he found a clean new ball,
carried it in saxophone

fingers, in his pocket now;
he feels the old jazz moving,

automatically grips
the hidden ball with the seams.

EASTER AFTERNOON SPLINTERED

Between network round ballers, grocery store,
A windy run through the bright green forest,

Kids outgrown colored eggs, baskets, bunnies,
Now clicked on to Nintendo Major League--

Yet, a slow hour
Before twilight we toss a baseball and
Bat it lightly toward the grassy field
Overgrown with purple flowers, fragrant
When you bend down to search an errant
Hit or a lost throw, beauty raw as the
Mountain, heavy in its four shades of
Evening green behind my twelve-year-old;
A father and two sons, we play together
In a warm resurrection of sunshine,
We connect with line drives of the heart,
So beyond the tomb of busy separation,
I watch the thin profile of my sixteen-
Year-old lope under a soft fly ball, his
Shadow barely a shadow, his long idle
Glove closing perfectly.

RIDING FRANK'S BIKE

Four months before cancer sucked him hollow,
Frank called me to get his stationary,
"Can't ride it anymore," he said, laying
His pipe on the dark red coffee table.

Frank had been my night auditor back in
The motel days, educated and tough,
The world slept easily while he labored
Through the years of protracted nights; mornings

I arrived to send him home where he watched
Baseball, rode the bike and dreamed of old days.
I carried the bike on my shoulder out
The front door, last time I saw Frank, alive.

Eight years later I pedal some evenings,
The odometer broken, square digits
Stuck on Frank's last efforts; my feet rise, then
Push down, while minutes pass, soon the circle

Turns more easily as if some extra
Feet were propelling me along.

MAURY'S METAPHORS

Every ugly coyote with an Acme
Bag of industrial tricks, hurling
Dynamite at his anchored knees—
Great pitchers sent diving foolishly,
Headlong over cliffs to early showers
By this "dodger"--

Up from "Twist," artful, menacing, that lead step
Money meant, no gaunt Fagen for control—
Old London or LA, a daring epic
All the same.

Before pool table infields and cement skies,
An eight ball, wild out of the back of the rack,
Wills, will, wheels.

SHADOWFAX

Get on that mound in LA if you don't
Think it's there—like a computer screen held
Too long, a burned image, barely visible:
A jet stream whispering through fragile clouds
Against a backdrop of bright summer blue—Dodger
blue.

Especially a lefty, on such a day
Blurs to the untrained eye, a blue shady
Outline tracks on an out-of-focus flick.

Get on that mound, if you don't believe
In Shadowfax. Kick your leg high into
A perfect peaceful sky and feel
The history ride right through you.

I GIVE YOU THE CHALKY TIPS OF MY FINGERS

Dry as an anthill in August, age steals
The romance from my skin, scaly arid,
Less powerful than when I gripped the red
Stitched seams of a summer baseball in what
Now seems a distant hazy dream, seems
Someone else's flight of fancy, not the
Man who races a marker across a
Whiteboard for two hours then fights to feel
Ambivalence toward creeping pain—

I give you splotchy discolored scarred flesh
Where my hands tried to stop me from breaking
A tooth, busting my chin, keeping head
Before heels, waving through unseen danger
In the air, upon the water, I watch
When I dream, have trained myself to see
A better, younger pair of hands than these
And yet, even as my finger tips glance
Across these keys, they grow chalky and numb—
They are not useful like old bricks, but please,
Take them anyway.

COMING HOME TO THE FIRE OF JULY

In air that may as well smoke itself
We stir like molten beings that
Must fight to maintain our shape—
The refrigerant, however, keeps
Us good for another day and the night
Finds us sluggish at the ballpark
Signaling the concessionaire perpetually.

Afterward,
Down by the lake that searches itself
For a better body to drown, out beyond
The hazy light of the narcotic moon
Where even the crickets quieten—
We threaten to stay
We threaten to call ourselves
Home to the water.

CALL HIM RED

The first person to teach me
About betting baseball—
He gambled every game day
While working the second shift
As clerk at an independent motel.

When the evening settled,
He'd sit, flip through pages
In his notebook of records
And tendencies—
"Always bet the streaks,"
He told me, flicking a loose strand
Of dark Vitalised hair
Back off his forehead.
"It's the nature of the game—"
Turning a page he'd note
The Orioles lack of speed on carpet,

Red always bet on the Dodgers,
Day after day, week into week,
Season into season.
"They never have a losing record,"
He said, though I suspected
They were just his favorites.
He had a nice car, lots of electronic
Toys, vast collections of old radio shows,
His other hobby.

The owners knew they paid him
Poverty wages, suspected, then fired Red
For concealing cash transactions,
A charge they "proved" by holding
Two similar daily records up to the light,
One damningly out of sync with the other.

He left pleasantly, collecting his recorders,
Radios, and miniature TV's.

"Focus on the good times," he said,
As if he knew Vonnegut,
Passing the last time out the front door.

Eighteen years have passed now,
Red became a salesman, I think.
Did well for a while, I heard.

Last winter his picture and column
Appeared in the local obituaries
Lost a close one to cancer
Before the games even started—
Like sad Lorca taking his bullet before
The first morning rays of sunlight
Could find him by the wall.

SPRING BASEBALL

Pitching in an icy breeze
My long blue sleeves I remember
Their juxtaposition against all the gray:
The low sky of heavy clouds,
The gray sandy base paths
That kicked up tiny gravel when I blinked
Or didn't, the gray faces of batters
Chopping through gray gusts of wind.

Toeing the worn gray rubber,
Raising my slender blue arms then
Swinging them back and
Kicking a black cleat into the silent heavens—
I still can feel
The first droplets of cold, dull rain.

THE MOON WRESTLES THE SKY AWAY

And you sit before the
Cold fact of the computer,
A hard cramp in your gut,
That game day feeling again
That once rendered you
All but speechless, monosyllabic,
Stunned as a rabbit you held
While your father
Sliced its white throat
And talked about the place of man--

You scraped the junior high mound
With a white cleat
Till it held your toe just right,
You heard the low buzz of the sparse crowd
As the crickets quietened in the kudzu
That ran the gut of the creek beyond left.
You caught the fuzzy signal from the catcher
And rocked into the windup just
As the moon wrestled the sky away.

IN A FIELD BESIDE MY DAD'S OLD HOME PLACE

We played ball most of the afternoon
While the adults and my oldest brother
Mowed the fields and cleaned out the
Tangled mess in the low land around
The clay-bottomed creek—
The sun baked us kids in July in rural Rowan County
But we played on with the bag of Little League bats
And gloves that Dad had stowed in the trunk
Of the '67 Chevy Bel Air, the first car we'd had
With actual air conditioning—
My cousins, the middle brother, and some
Neighborhood kids that had arrived
On rusty bicycles with tattered banana seats
Battled the hours, the chiggers--both teams
Wanting to be the Braves, maybe one renegade
With a vacant look and a bad crew cut
That called for the Dodgers—
Now and then there would be an argument
Over a call at first or whether a fly ball
Really cleared the cedar in center that
Served as a fence and a warning for
A real barbed wire fence—
The scores grew into the forties and fifties
Before calls of supper scattered us
To our respective appetites—
There was always another day that week
Of what my Dad called vacation—
Nights we listened to the feint radio signal
Of a Braves broadcast that left as much
To our imaginations as it gave us—
The next day we were ready, however,
With fresh ideas of heroism and the game.

DAD STEPPED OFF THE MOUND

Assuring us his feet were exactly
A foot in length, the line corn row straight—
Anywhere we went, vacation or what-
Ever, Paul and I waited for those careful steps,
Pirouetting in practice windup kicks,
Slamming ball to glove, ball to glove, while bees
Danced through the clover of the 1960's.

Dad stepped off the mound, a cap yanked tightly
Over his bald head, marching then like a
Baseball soldier back behind the freshly
Established plate, our anticipation
Always fresh as forty-six soon became
Sixty and a half and sunny summers
Silently slipped away.

GRAY AREA

Streaking ghost that moved casually, Pete Gray,
While THE BIG ONE raged toward finality,
And the factories churned unblinkingly,
Before Robinson, before Roseboro,
Pete cracked another barrier, one-armed
Overcome by fleet footed fielding when
Every man had to give what he had to
Give, Pete sent many thanking the Lord
For right arms—for symmetry—the rest
Just went on, hard and gray as Russia
On a flickering newsreel, while Pete
Smiling, took the St. Louis field.

HARRY SWINGS THE HAMMER

Down in Florida, rumpled as Columbo,
His voice batters you like a gavel—
Sarasota summers, little league ball,
A lesser man might be squelched by the heat.
Not Harry in black mask and blue shirt, crouched
Over the catcher's right shoulder, "bullring eyes"
Measuring the corner—"STIRRRIKE" in a dull
Scotch-Irish growl, his iambic moment
Punctuated by a parent's loud curse,
Harry's heavy thumb rises up like a sledge.
Trained at Duke in law, instead, the evening
Arbiter rules this coastal court, Harry
Brody, the poet-umpire calls 'em
JUST, like He seeees 'em.

THE DYNAMIC OF THE FOLDED CARDS IN THE
SEVENTH INNING—

Eight runs behind and so what has been
Sent to the bombed out mound with his six point
Something ERA and his mental issues—

Rain would be way too late and the Groundskeep
Rallies his guys by the tarps and wishes
It were over, wanting a cigarette,
Posing like he has one, a leg resting
On the first step of the left field bleacher—

The thick-necked manager loses, placid
As a grazing cow, his huge bovine head
Leaned against the dugout wall behind the
Bench where his players are bored with looking
For women in the box seats, most of them
Bored also but free to leave to bars and
Grills, the types of which have mushroomed out
By the drive to the stadium where players
Know they can find the half-hearted win
Of them later.

KILLEBREW

Harmon, whose bat sang such sweet melodies
To hoarse fans with teeth still clenched from
Fallen mercury, who slid fast into wooden-
Slatted seats that thawed a blessed month
Later each year. Harmon, built more like a
Viking than a Twin, kept their ship arace
With a sharp eye instead of a sharp axe,
Harmon, who burst through the ice that freezes
The heart there in Minnesota.

WATCHING AARON RUN AT THE STATE TRACK MEET

Just like my dad, I wanted him to pitch.
Tall and limber, strong-armed and smart, he quit
the game earlier than I.

Now here under pine trees in Raleigh's heat
we wait in slouch chairs, sipping drinks, as the
swelter turns to storm then stops.

When he was six, he hit homeruns and
fielded second with grace and guts. He was
the next big thing in a family

stranded in the muck of potential,
redemption for the woes I'd given
my dad, for the chances he never had.

Now I wait for this red-haired gazelle
who takes the hollow plastic baton at
the careful start of his leg, fiery-eyed, he catches

his heart on the back-stretch, holding his own against
the best. I feel the tension in my hands where I grip
the metal fence I have come to.

Leaning hard forward, he passes the handoff, having
relayed this family of vicarious hard ballers further
than it could ever deserve.

PEDRO'S MAJIK

The pitcher's road is scored
by the message of his face.

As **you** come set,
your face reveals nothing,

a curtain drawn on the
fact of fans.

You could be listening
for the tick of a turning lock,

for the last jar of green beans
to seal.

A gunfighter's eyes, so sure
you've got the goods:

that your curve will dip
like a fork
into a pickle jar;

that your fastball will always be
a cold steel beam
in the mud hut
of all these hitters.

STRUCK OUT ON MAIN STREET

The old man staggered toward me
like he was moving through snow.

Mom had sent us to collect him
from the pool hall, the last thing

to do before supper and a little
league ball game at the town park.

My brother Bill and me grabbed him
like we usually did, one under each arm.

Only a block and a half to the house,
we didn't want to be late; it was a big game.

Pop was heavier than usual, not gliding
to some honky tonk song he hummed.

When he fell into the street, I hoped a
cop would come along; we couldn't go home

without him. He smelled like car oil and
shaving cream and puke, and I could see

the blood begin down the side of his face
where he hit the pavement.

Drag and wobble, drag and wobble; nobody
stopped to help us; we were Lineberger boys;

it was our job to get the old man home.
Late for the game, the coach kept me out

till the third; we lost.
Afterward, Bill and me sat in playground

swings and smoked the cigarettes we'd took
from the old man's pocket.

The moon was gone, and it was the clearest,
darkest night I can ever remember.

THE UNIT PAINTS THE BIG SKY OF WORDS

He paints the big sky of words with pitches,
a sweeping arm long enough to lie, then
tell the truth in sixty blinding feet.

The batter waits in an unbalanced stance
like a swimmer in shark infested water,
listening through the melody of fear.

Johnson paints the big sky with leather smacked,
the executioner's measuring eyes,
and all the blue silence between the roars.

SEVEN HUNDRED MPH FASTBALL

The baseball burns right through our hearts:
stands empty, stadiums dark.
The September sideshow on hold,
the air is still; the night is cold.

WHITEWASH

He had been your favorite for years,
a country boy with a big swing
and a Hollywood grin.

Like yours, his father drove
a truck, ran a part-time farm,
so you cheered his flaming throws
to second, the moments his bat
owned every fan's fluttering stomach.

Twelve years and he was now
an old dog with a sure spot in the Hall,
and you a beer mellowed hotel clerk
when you saw him out by third base
at a game in Atlanta.

When you hollered from Fulton County's vacant
boxes, he cursed you in reply,
Like three quick lashes of the whip,
his words fell against the putty of your face.

You could not have known anything
beyond the interview-ese of this "kindred spirit,"
how he lived between the flash of cameras, the
broken creep of pain in his every step.

All you knew was the bile brought
to your dry mouth and the hatred that grew
with every step that took you back to the seats you
could afford.

PILLS THAT ONCE STRUNG ME OUT

now keep me moving,
now widen the groove of my reach,
now settle my eye like the sun
over the stadium roof.

Today I run out
from under anvils,
take the base paths
on rocket skates.

A veteran is a package of secrets,
so I dress early,
leave quickly before the flashes
find these craters,
this foxhole kicked wide,

before a bungled autograph,
before the blonde groupie
can wait
for my sting.

The field is not a stage,
and I am not ready
for crosswords or to be one;
one shake of this bottle—
and you will see
how steady I get.

GIBBY

A lean black temple of big hands,
hard flashing eyes, to his task
connected like
a heart is connected to music,
a task no one could do
like he could, a labor of hate,
guarding the brown hill,
sure every batter could raise
him to Golgotha, if he dared
drop the whip of his inside pitch,
or turn the notch of intensity
down.

In '68, his ERA on the head
of a pin, at thirty-two,
a midwestern god not so far
from home, too tall, it would
seem, for a tall mound,
profane and graceful,
mean and precise,
elegant as the distant
river jazz, yet surely
but slowly sinking
like the moon into the
heavy water.

DODGERS-BRAVES, 66
A Man's Lesson

There are two outs,
Bottom of the ninth,
Bases empty,
Braves trailing 2-0.

I am nine years old
Listening to Dad's old radio
And Koufax is pitching,
Lanky, quiet Sandy;
His fastball has
Eaten the edge off
The plate all evening.
The Braves have one hit,
A weak infield grounder.

With two strikes
Alou swings at a low fast one
The catcher slaps to the dirt,
And Felipe
Hustles out of the box
Crossing first just after
The fielder muffs
The catcher's wide throw.

The few, the proud
Stir in their blue seats.
I roll over on my elbow
In the bed.

Felix "the Cat" Millan,
Short of stature,
The Braves second sacker
Steps in, digs in,
Crowds his heart
Out over the dish and waits

As Sandy, a sure
Surgeon all night
Can not measure him
And soon sends him
Along with Alou to the pond.
No crowd to roar
For Sandy had sent them
Up and down 85 long ago.

In '66 Atlanta
This game matters not,
Yet I am up against the pillow
Leaning, listening to
Milo Hamilton thinking
Out loud the
Unthinkable,
"What if Henry...?"

Then Aaron sets himself
As he did,
The bat propped against
One hip
As he pats the helmet
With both powerful hands
Till it sticks where it already was

And fixes his feet
The width of his shoulders
And wags his bat
With those awesome wrists,
Till the pitch streaks
Toward the plate
So fast he can hear it

Then, Milo, nearly
Hysterical,
"there's a drive, way
back, way back, it's
outta here, it's outta

here---the Braves
have beaten the Dodgers,
the Braves have beaten
the Dodgers!

I have seen miracles since,
The hopeless rising somehow,
The ill fighting for
Another inning of life,
At times felt struck out myself
Till I remember
Alou running struck out for first
Through the radio waves
And the August heat
On a worn out radio
In an upstairs bedroom
In a church parsonage
Where a nine year-old boy,
The only one awake
In the house,
Learned a man's lesson.

DNA

Papaw balanced peas on a knife.
Daddy threw a string ball he'd made
Against the barn. Grandma lay dying
In a back room of the farmhouse.
The cows drank water in the feed lot.
The other kids all grown and gone
Except little sister Ginny,
A blue shadow in the stale kitchen.
Daddy who had waited and waited,
Holding a warm cloth to Grandma's face,
Went out to "pitch" and chat with God
When he felt his mother
Sweep right through him.

"DON'T LOOK BACK"

The great Satchel Paige always said,
But as a runner I've learned to sneak
A glance across a pivoting shoulder
Like a swimmer drawing breath—
And when a pitcher I recall some similar
Movement of the eyes toward a runner
Dancing from the base--

A lesson I have learned and relearned,
Paranoid though it may seem,
Do Look Back!
At work, at play,
The shotgun barrel is lowering
Across your back as you relax—
Behind the smiles that met you
So casually, so sincere—
The snarling teeth are bared,
The slashing claws are coming—

Participant in life, beware!
Do Look Back!
The strong grow stronger,
And you couldn't be wronger
To pause and savor this affair!

A FADED PHOTO OF A DISTANT YEAR

We have given up resemblance
to any young man's smile or hard
baseball look. Our eyes are gone
under cap bills bent in the
kids' fashion of the past.

That hot summer day now just a
forgotten tick on a bigger clock—
two flanneled rows of undefeated
little leaguers, never came to run
this town; instead we took our places

through the droning years in factories
like our fathers, skillful,
diligent, accepting the hand dealt,
the faith of our grandfathers and theirs—
look now, how you could see it
even then.

1945

The boys returned from France
and Italy and the Pacific
to smaller, meaner ball fields,
too big for their towns,
too old or torn up
for the teams they left.
They flocked to the colleges,
to the married housing,
aged men with their lives
laid out before them,
thinking of businesses,
optimistic leaders
of the whole free world,
men convinced a God
had spared them
for something more
than a job at the mill,
men hungry to catch up
with time, with families,
willing to leave the ball games
to the boys they'd left behind.

THAT DAY

1948, the July sun burns
out Main Street past the theaters,
one billed with a western, the other, war—
three PM, brick veneered storefronts catch fire
for a moment; then wind catches the yellow
dresses of two women waiting at the corner
by the hotel for minor league players,
for a glimpse of the Cuban pitcher.

Dusty black cars creep by
to give the new stoplights business;
the Baptist church chimes the dry hour—
a small town with a spring loaded future,
a sewer system and a good river.
4 PM, Pat's Cab carries the Cuban
and the women away, his fastball, he
will remember, was hot enough for both, that day.

AMERICANA

Ride blue two lanes into twilight,
up through the flat slab of Tennessee.
Climb the blasted granite hills of Kentucky,
winding toward the crown at the Ohio.

Could be forty-nine, could be fifty,
the Packard limousine hums hard.
Hank leans into a coil of cigarette smoke,
white Stetson pulled eyebrow low.

His free hand stabs the radio buttons;
tonight he's got the Sox, the Dodgers,
the Tigers: three games he follows
in three minute listens, song length segments

that drive young Jerry Rivers crazy at the wheel,
lost without a fiddle against his shoulder;
and who could really know
what Hank thinks as the miles

roll under the innings, lost himself
in pitches and checked swings,
stolen bases and triples, sanctuary
from the demons that haunt

the next hotel room, the waves of faces
that love him too much,
all the bitter cracks in all the walls.
Ride blue two lanes into twilight,

up through the flat slab of Tennessee;
in the rearview, the pain grows bright lights.
On the radio the Tigers are winning, the Sox
are losing and the Dodgers remain tied.

GOD IS RAIN

On a night when
silence is a gun held
against the staccato tick
of the clock you would dismiss
from its paneled height, the
blues are the last thing
that catch you,
catch you like water
at the circular base
of this Saturday,
catch you
like Salinger's graceless boy,
in a moonlit field gone gray,
catch you
like Willie Mays, deep in center,
running hard as a storm;
God is rain.

THE FAT MAN AT THE BALL PARK

Geoff's second wife was Romanian, a beauty
with a small pointed nose like a fox,
greenish brown eyes and long slim legs.
Geoff was gaunt-faced and dark bearded,
dressed in flannel and jeans, black boots,
a red ball cap always pulled to his brow.

He met her at the community college,
fresh from her homeland, enrolled in
a radiography program.
He could barely believe his luck,
often pondered his worthiness,
she'd come here, a lottery visa winner,

but he felt like the lottery winner
tracing the curve of her back, late at night,
listening to stories of back home.
The baseball game was his idea,
a local minor league team; she sat
and read a foreign novel while he

munched on peanuts, hollered
at batters and pitchers, and drank
a bit too much. He was a poet of sorts
who often wrote about the game
and had a small reputation for his work.
When she caught him staring up at the

bleachers, her face soured; "That girl
can't be more than thirteen," she said,
referring to the young girl in short shorts
midriff displayed, talking on a cell phone.
"I'm watching the fat man; I'm going
to write a poem about him, the fat man

who's always up there in that same spot."
"Why a fat man?" she asked, turning a page

in her novel. "He's always there, wearing
that same dark blue Yankees cap, holding
his scorecard, shifting uncomfortably
on the metal seat; he's poetic, don't you see?"

When the foul ball smacked Geoff, it was a direct hit,
a nineteen year-old Puerto Rican's slow bat
slicing through the zone a micro-second late.
It took eight stitches to sew his cheek up;
the baseball seams left red marks
that finally went away in six months.

The next season, after his second wife
had left him, he went back to the park.
The fat man was still there in the same seat,
wearing his dark blue Yankees cap,
carefully keeping his game card, a bit
heavier maybe; he couldn't decide.

THE HUNTER SEES THE WORLD
for John Billy

Sitting on the porch deck at his cabin,
he scans the trees, the field below.

With him I have walked streets
in Detroit, Denver, Atlanta;

sixty-five, right hand in pocket
gripping a knife, his eyes intense.

Sixty-six, chasing me corner to
tennis court corner, gray-haired,

rough-faced as Bukowski, relentless.
Sixty-seven, retired from the classroom

he managed like a ship, barking, bantering,
perfect grammar, careful annunciation.

Early fall evening on the deck, rifle across
his lap, a sweaty glass of bourbon in hand,

fourth inning of the ballgame on the radio
when the groundhog makes his move.

EIGHT HUNDRED LIVING PIRATES

There are eight hundred living Pirates
all across the land, says Nellie Briles,
the white-haired, portly hot stove speaker.

Full of chicken and anecdotes, I imagine
them, eye-patched, rum-drunk in Carolina,
scoping the pitching Atlantic for a black flag;

swaggering to casinos in Biloxi,
across white gulf sand in Panama hats,
aging, still slugger-shouldered;

hunkered down in townhouses on South Beach,
secluded with gold rings and loot,
game tapes and silver bats;

eight hundred living swash bucklers,
Manny and Matty, Willie and Big Bob,
Kent and Danny, Magical Maz—

the list goes on till Briles
with his rich Roberto imitation
brings one more great one back to life.

JESSE WILLIS, HARD AND LOW

He was tautly-muscled by work,
ground down by the chase,
raccoon-eyed by shadows,
storming toward the grave.

His old Ford pickup, a
growling gray-primered ghost,
his woman, a black-rooted,
tired, skinny, slapped blonde,

He was savoring the burn
of liquor in his throat,
steering Greedy's Highway
with one meaty hand,

pounding to a Drive-By Truckers
song, Skynyrd, watch out oak tree
guitars and such, the night one
big dark beautiful beast.

He was not thinking
about school clothes his kids needed,
about building furniture frames,
about the scholarship he passed on,

or the way the world once looked
from a pitcher's mound.
He was not thinking
of doctors' daughters

or their spreading cheerleader legs;
he was wholly without
hatred or fear or dreams of
chains and cages.

He was, however, raccoon-eyed
by shadows like a pitcher
in a fast sunny game, his cap
pulled down hard and low.

44

I THOUGHT I KNEW WHEN CHILDHOOD ENDED

When we hung up the gloves
and the ball grew dusty
in the corner,
I thought childhood had ended.
When we drove to drive-ins,
with girls curled
like cats in back seats,
I thought childhood had ended.
When college called
and we answered the books
with caffeine and marijuana,
I thought childhood had ended.
When we married the ones
who accepted our secrets
and forgave us our pasts,
I thought childhood had ended.
When our own kids toddled and spit,
then hoofed it
off to play school,
I thought childhood had ended.
When we protected them,
coaxed them, and begged them
to be just like us,
I thought childhood had ended.
When they left, too,
fuzzy futures, born like sacks
across their shoulders,
I "knew" childhood had ended.
Yet, last night, after a sunny day
of pitching mindlessly through
eighteen innings, eighteen holes,
his cancerous body anchored in that "bed of awe,"
Coffey left us at the hospice
to remember golden summers
on red dirt diamonds, to sniff
freshly cut fescue on the links,

and finally to know
that childhood only ends
when one loses
his childhood friends.

SHERRY

Two boys, one to hit, and one to field,
then to switch. She'd mapped the yard
and knew where the bushes were,
where the clothesline ran.
Her back to the plate, she marked off
this year's spot with confident steps,
turned till the sun glinted off
the thick shades she'd worn
since she left the hospital,
since her husband slammed
her into the stone fireplace,
destroying her eyes.
She felt the seams of the ball,
aligning them with her first two fingers.
She knew the boys' height
from hugging them every day.
She knew how to come forward
and when to let go.
She knew to duck
but would sometimes
get hit by grounders.
Sherry threw strikes
that only her sons could see.
No wonder they became
all-star players.
No wonder they became
good men.

CLOYD HAGER

It's 1928 and he's reaching for a throw
in a college annual pose, third baseman
in the bloom of youth with an empty
grassy field stretching fence-ward far behind him.

He is big, hungry, and fearless;
long sleeves under the gray flannel
suggest early March, the turf still rough
from autumn's football struggles.

He could be any country tough guy,
rawboned, red-cheeked, yet noble,
Germanic, Irish, or both, eyes
on the ball, reaching for the sky.

In '41, a mill town high school principal,
he'll stop by a roadside fruit stand,
to pick up some fresh tomatoes
to take home to his new wife.

And while he fans himself with his hat,
holding his suit jacket under one arm,
the teenage vendor will tell him how
he wants to go into the ministry.

Later that weekend he will call the mill owner
to tell him about the ambitious farm boy-
and he will send my dad to Cloyd's college
where he will soon meet my mother.

COACH DAD

He had a theory about losing,
about the absence of dwelling on,
of brooding over failure,
hours he spent proving
on hard packed school yard fields
with a bushel of cheap Haitian balls,
a half dozen taped together bats,
two beaten helmets that had to fit
over goofy ears and knotty heads,
yet hitting the cutoff, backing
the bases, and learning to bunt
were what mattered when the
city park lit up and the parents
slid their lawn chairs
against the chicken wire backstop,
smoking Winstons and Lucky Strikes,
shouting their own impatient theories
as a summer storm gathered
over the unfathomable night.

AMERICAN TROPHY

First it was speed and skill,
a postcard swing, the heel turned elegantly,
enveloping the great ocean of center field,
dodging through pin striped ghosts till
the whole island re-grew nine flags
under you, nine rings for men to rule.

Then every Manhattan eatery craved
your jacket, tie, soft-spoken appearance,
discretion with the ladies, their stars
the bargain and you a streak that could
never be broken, the world forever
aflame for a cooled piece of your meteor.

Traded the bay for Ruth's yard, finally
the signing dirges, whole days
to avenge "what they did to you,"
gray and proper as a count,
Frisco catholic dropout, sweet paranoid
grandfather, slaying dragons with your pen.

COFFEY ON HIS FORTY-NINTH

A ghost crosses the fast moving water
of this night, early April, my old friend's
forty-ninth birthday, so I think of his life,
again, to keep him alive a while longer,

to beat the cancer of time, its poppy field
of forgetfulness. Tim, who squeezed
his considerable story into 46 years
of action, who worked the two jobs,

who refereed and umpired, played
his beloved golf, who had the greatest
smile ever as Coach Barnes noted at the
funeral where beautiful women

gathered to miss his charisma forever.
Long years since red dirt little league
baseball, seven different fearless
slides, escaping the befuddled rundown,

the scrawny catcher with a rocket arm.
Time, time, and my dad who coached him
and loved him like a fourth son, gone, too.
A ghost crosses the fast moving water.

For a moment, I go under in the night,
into the bobbing jack spin of an eddy,
becoming a part of the river that runs
through here over and over, then I rise.

MASTERMIND

A keg of gray slump-shouldered redneck,
ruddy-faced, the Red Skelton version
of misdiagnosed genius, and oh that
dugout voice rising like a drawn knife
in the Georgian world, Bermuda high
that might stifle a lesser man, one not so
God blessed with Joneses, replacement
surgeries, empiric tendencies. Every
year a haggard naysayer start followed by
a gold bond finish, a simple recipe
for the ages: different last legged washouts,
a dandy crop grown close to the vine,
Joneses, the Michigan militia,
a keg of redneck horse farm brilliance,
the sky flagged one more time.

ONLY IN AMERICA

Maybe you dream
and watch the rocking curve of the earth,
despising the smell of fish.
Maybe your father takes you
to Yankee Stadium on Sundays
to see the great Dimaggio.
Maybe you swing
from the heels, glide across Frisco sandlots
besting your talented brothers.
Maybe you team
with an angel-voiced hipster, stirring
American nostalgia with your words.
Maybe you rule
the kingdom of baseball, cat powerful, cool
glamorous grace in the gossips.
Maybe you wonder out loud where Joltin' Joe has
gone, though it's really about you.
Maybe you age
in the spotlight of handshake and card show
lines, constructing the grandkids' trusts.
Maybe you wander
on your own through unsettled decades,
school yards, grace lands, dreams of summer.
Maybe you die
one month short of opening day,
convinced that Marilyn awaits you.
Maybe you return to Yankee Stadium on Joe's day,
packed house, stand in center field and sing "Mrs.
Robinson."

NOW YOU GOT 'EM WHERE YOU WANT 'EM

Nobody told us
The proper way to fall off the mound
In position to field; our junior high coach
Was a seventh grade history teacher
Ironically named John McGraw,
A fact you could not make up,
And our workhorse pitcher was a
Bullet-headed lefty from Rhode Island
Whose main claim to fame
Was his John Kennedy "It's my ball;
We play by my rules" imitation
Which none of us dumb hicks
Ever really got, and the only time
He wasn't running his mouth
Was when he was pitching
And his batting practice tosses
Came screaming back at him as he
Stumbled off to the right of the mound
Leaning over like someone
Looking for a contact lens
And the "Little Napoleon" McGraw
Would shove his stubby hands
Deeper into his windbreaker pockets
And holler "Good job, George.
Now you got 'em where you want 'em."

1961

The dirt is whiter, sandier than home
and there's the slightest breeze stirring the pines.
The men have removed their suit jackets,
their white shirts sweated around the arm pits.
They sit on lawn chairs, the old metal kind,
dark green and pitched forward just a little.
They hold their hats in their laps and tell
stories about the church or the mill or the farm.
They laugh and one of them turns the crank on an
ice cream maker, tapping a black brogan on a tree
root.

I am four, and too young to play ball, have been
convinced to sit on a towel atop the churn.
I smile and smell peaches, listen to an uncle's
lazy, hypnotic voice, his comment about the heat.
It will always be like this, I think, summer afternoons,
a baseball game playing on a transistor,
the whole cocoon of family.

IS THERE NOTHING?

Is there nothing for feet that hurt like this?
For the hammer jarred elbow and taut wrist?
I think of my brother who picks splinters
From forty-something fingers, silently
Ages in the frame shop dust and cruel heat—

I think of my brother, who played first base,
Half-deaf, innocent as a mule to the
Wants of the future, left-handed and strong,
My brother whose backyard pitches to Dad
Never took him to a real childhood mound—
My brother who took the mean punches
Of playground ridicule and indifference,
Drove nails into the wood of invention,
Hammering the darkness back, year after year,

Today I lean into a wooden lectern,
Stare at a yawning class, hearing their deep,
Numbing breath,
And think of my steady hardworking brother,
The priority of his pain, and the
Fast rule of silence.

CALLOUSED KID HANDS

I remember my hair
clipped like the yellow stubble
in the autumn field
after a haying.

Our clothes were
always Sears/Roebuck,
ordered in August
for a new year of school.

We ate home cooked,
fresh from the garden
after a cool July
thunderstorm.

The black and white
had rabbit ears
we moved to sharpen
the fuzz from Charlotte.

Meat close to the bone,
we lived the summer
on red dusty ball fields
clutching oiled gloves

we had carefully chosen
along with white ash
bats, gripped by
callused kid hands,

hands that learned young
how to hold on
to what is fine
in this sweet world.

I SINK INTO THIS PILLOW

I sink into this pillow
that cannot contain
the itch of this April evening.

Across town,
my childhood friend waits
for the operation of the morning,
for the gloved hands
that will or will not evict death,
a recent, unwelcome stranger
from his colon.

Rather than in fast and prayer,
I think of him instead,
the dark haired kid of barefoot summers,
our undersized catcher at ten,
chattering in a husky man's voice
as the ace delivered a concoction
of crooked pitches which he caught
without benefit of signals;
I think of his dark radar eyes,
his small precise hands, of
how we were convinced
he could see the future.

I sink in this pillow now,
as drivers cruise dark highways
beyond my window,
playing the mysterious music
of their own uninterrupted lives.

58

MY DAD ON HIS 78th

The veils are drawn back again,
his teary voice let go,
a voice that once uttered
unfalteringly, the last
fearsome words over the dead.

Melancholy minus the holy;
that's how this feels as
I slip him an audio book
he wanted, and a card
with its stupid pointless joke.

He could leave our game today,
take the intentional walk,
but the chairs in this stank room
are bases loaded with the
gravity of grandchildren.

MY FATHER'S 80th BIRTHDAY

On the mountain or a mound,
to rise above the clatter,
to think as I move—hunt or
be hunted, kill or be killed.

This day has consequences;
the cat comes down the sidewalk,
mouse in mouth, watching a bird.
The drizzle blesses my sneeze.

The afternoon is a book
of grass and humidity
I read over and over,
then mark my place with death.

Death stops birthdays, it would seem,
the only mercy on earth.
His fresh grave is a mound I
recite Dickinson over.

HAMMERED, 1952

He said it was a sound
he'd never forget.
The team had swung north
from Winston, stopping
in Richmond and then
on to Washington where
they filled the stadium
for an afternoon double header,
were taken to a DC diner for dinner
where they ate quietly
in the wide-eyed customer glare,
wiped their tired faces and rested
while the kitchen workers cursed
and crashed dishes into metal
containers rather than reuse
what colored hands had lay on,
and he knew that if they
had fed stray dogs with those plates
they would have washed them.

Just a skinny black kid
a long way from Mobile,
he folded and refolded his napkin
as cheap china smashed the silence
and he kept his eyes down on
the checkered tablecloth.

ONE THEORY

So here it is:
some horribly ill-fitted analogy,
television, the dragon that came
and stayed for supper, Jack Crack
and his intestines looped over Mexico
while the corn grew tall near Trap Hill
and the best the girls could do
was the home town's Brando,
Kid Korea, returning from a hitch
to pitch Class D Ball, who
already knew there's nothing
to win, nearly nothing to lose,
that tonight can't do
a damn thing for tomorrow.
So when the game tanked,
the frontier lost its best
box of tools and the bad boys
stood up like the worst bunch
of struck out kings, waving
like the sheepishly drunken
Jack Crack out behind Mama's
in a broken down lawn chair
and who could have known
what he saw or was
in Rocky Top as slow pitch
softball vaguely began
to weave the Internet.

OLD MAN POEMS 1

I'd lay my pipe on the table beside the chair
And get on the exercise bike
That had belonged to one of the Clydes.
It was the best thing for the cancer,
The doctor told me. After a while
I could go five miles, sometimes
Twice in one day, and I'd watch
A Braves game while I pedaled
Or listen to music on the headphones
Cause otherwise my wife'd try to talk
And a man with cancer hasn't got time
To talk while he's riding a bicycle
That is taking him nowhere.

OLD MAN POEMS 2

It was the year I hit
A blackjack home run in June
And the cab drivers that gambled
Out by left field brought me
A shoe box half full of dollar bills.
Nights I wasn't chasing something else,
I'd go home to the house we'd rented
On the mountain, and she'd fetch beers
To the back porch where we'd watch
The lights across the valley
And I'd tell her the lie I'd told ten years,
How we were gonna make it to the show.
But the Class D was all too easy:
The daddy spanked Baptist town girls,
The one pitch country farm hands,
And though my swing busted everything,
My boyfriend shot left foot staggered me,
Caged me, destroyed my soul.
Class D, and the D stood for despair.

AFTER GOD 45

The slowest time ever
Was when he had the ball in his hand,
Nodding leisurely to the coiled catcher,
Waiting for the batter to set,
And he focused on nothing but the mitt,
And there would never be another time
In his life when the immediate world
Stood still waiting for him to swing
His lanky arms up, and far into
Adulthood he would recall
Every smell, sound, the dreamy
Sensation of release, the last time
He knew we are not all alone
In this universe.

WILD IN THE STRIKE ZONE, 2007

I had heard about him for a couple years,
A co-worker told me his daughter who
Tutored him in math went to watch and said,
Daddy, when he throws the ball,
You can hear it singing through the air,
So I left work early, carried my slouch chair
From the high school parking lot
Down a path that led to a red dirt hillside
Overlooking a modest ball field
Where soon every possible open space
Featured a lawn chair or blanket of people,
And I perched awkwardly, a face among faces
As he warmed up, taller than expected,
Long-armed, blazing his pitches,
And I convened silently there
Amidst talk of radar guns
And cheerleader tryouts and all sorts of
Ho-hum as they were used to the thwack
Of David LePrevost's mitt, Madison's strikeouts,
His ridiculous location; they were
As unaffected as him, having seen
Years of it, and they already knew
Before he became
What he would become.

THE TIGERS ARE WINNING

My dad quit calling me after he died;
No more baseball discussions,
State of the family announcements,
He is just as dead as Faulkner or Freud
Or any Kennedy, but he was just a minister,
Grew up on a farm, listening to ball games
In the neighbor's milk barn.
Tonight I miss him because
His team, the Tigers, is winning,
And his absence is remarkable
Though not quite ironic.
Seven miles east of here, Dad's house sits in
This same southern storm, his recliner gone,
Thunder rolling through the October sky.
The Tigers are winning,
But there will be no phone call tonight.

2. OUTLAWS

THE BALLAD OF ALABAMA PITTS
the gospel of no forgiveness

Forgiveness begins somewhere, maybe when
the sun that pierces Sing Sing trims its heat
on the Umbrellaed avenues of Our
Country 'tis of thee--great land of freedom.
Beginning at one shore, forgiveness slides
like the sun that offers no restraint.

But fate works overtime under the skin
and some of us never feel that star stir
the first shadows of morning, the last flick
of dusk and its hard curtain, the cosmic
curtain of no forgiveness is all.

. . . .

Edwin Pitts, come from Alabama to Navy then New
York, then robbery, Sing Sing--no more than a farm
boy, found sports could scratch his itch
to catch the light beyond the bars, outside
the nation sprang from windows, then chopped roads
through woods over mountains, working from camps
like some kind of new soldiers, though fresh war
beckoned from the future, today was bread
and milk, the simple joy of sugar
or Sunday chicken--the importance that
poverty makes of food--Alabama,
The pride of Sing Sing, of open field runs
and running catches, of track star glory,
Alabama waited, for a pitch, for
parole, and a horsehide contract promised

by Evers, yes, second base Chicago Cub
Evers who fought like he fought in his day
of play for Pitts and his Albany club,
International League rehabilitation.

69

But a cloud swept across the sky, as Judge
Branham who ruled the circuit of the minors
pledged his denial to the convict; then
papers conscripted this "hero," hatched their spins--
and a nation, starved for diversion
chose quick sides, buzzed and rang with headstrong
versions and reasons--Pitts now, not Pitts ball-
player, but Pitts, cause celebre,
Pitts, poster-boy for society's hopes,
Sing Sing prison's greatest athlete felt
like a knight unarmored--yet enamored.

That coast to coast cry rang for justice,
for a second chance that America claimed
back to the full boat of its pilgrim roots--
and the pages dripped with give-the-boy
a-chance ink, when sports writers wrought art from
the occasion of their stories, broad-stroked
descriptions and heart string arguments made--
while Negroes played on in cold shadows, the
papers raised Pitts to their shoulders.

Football teams made gridiron proposals,
Dizzy Dean wrote, Pepper Martin sent word--
Warden Lawes of Sing Sing worked endlessly
till finally the mountain moved, Judge Landis
of major league commission, overruled,
canceling the lesser Branham, president
of mere minor leagues, and Pitts, ball player-
pawn regained a spot at Albany with
"Restrictions."

Irony it seemed would rule the bright day
when Pitts, who five years 'fore held a gun
in a grocery store, now held the eyes
of seven thousand happy fans and moved them
when he moved, but the waters of Albany
were deep, and the hero faltered in the
field and at the plate--over his head, the

70

newsmen said. Football and another year
were the same, no Sing Sing success outside
the walls, his, the fate of almost greatness.

The money running low, attention spent,
Pitts, the ex-con became Pitts the outlaw,
a star player in the Carolina League,
he tore it up for Charlotte, for Gastonia--
became a regular guy as well
working as a textile knitter, marrying,
starting a family while the games played on,
the money not bad, he settled in
Valdese, the Waldensian haven in tough
Burke County, North Carolina.

When the league went under, Pitts scrambled
to play, a shot here, a shot there,
never the glare of that spotlight again
till fate found him at a Valdese tavern
in '41, tapping the shoulder of a dancer
to cut in, a certain LeFevers who
took offense and a blade to Pitts,
the artery in his strong shoulder
spewing life out at thirty-one,
Sing Sing's greatest athlete gone.

JOE

A wolf ain't nothing but a dog gone bad,
gone bad and can't go back.

A mere boy who left the hard labor
of cotton mills and green southern fields, reluctantly,
uneducated and intuitive,
always suspicious of the letters laid
in black inky rows, everywhere.

He figured the pictures and reactions in faces
and hit the ball farther than anybody before,
a swing like the wolf's whole howl,
a heavy bat lifted to the sky, to the moon.

Never fit in Mack's Philly,
outfield or locker room, where the bumpkin jokes
ran like knives, hard into him.

Then Cleveland, by Eerie,
where his caring wife read him
the new tide of praise;
was a sweet tune, a melody
of triples and running catches,
smiling kids, endorsements, adulation,

but a wolf ain't nothing but a dog gone bad,
and Joe, off season
flew to the stage,
a flask in pocket, a beauty by each side,
memorizing the jokes, the smoke
and the lights of New Orleans
till the wife filed papers.

Another trade, another city by a lake,
the star of Charley's all-stars,
more glory, fast days, fierce throws
from the fence, towering drives

beyond it.

Then whispers, like the wind slipping
through wheat, a series blown,
while the lost generation
slid toward Paris, Jackson got drunk
and went to a hearing,
damned from the fields
he patrolled like a lion;
eleven seconds of death
hung from him as he walked
from the building to the car
past the say it ain't so's.

Blame Mr. Comiskey for squeezing his dollar,
blame that mere boy who left the hard labor
of cotton mills and green southern fields
if you will.
A wolf ain't nothing but a dog gone bad.

ALABAMA PITTS, WHO

who played without underwear
and slid hard on packed Piedmont dirt,
soaked strawberries with toilet paper
and spoiled the home team's rally
with a running catch;

who preferred Ed over his
celebrity convict nickname
but answered to anything
and took it from the wolves
like the Negroes would in ten years;

who tried it in the northeast but
landed in the south when he
couldn't hit the curve,
couldn't throw from the fence,
couldn't be the next Speaker;

who couldn't shake his mother,
even when he settled in Valdese,
married, coached the high school;
she was always lurking, scaring
his wife, his baby daughter;

who liked to party, liked the women;
nice, they said, though dark and brooding
when the big time never happened,
and outlaws and mill ball were
the Depression's solution.

who fought with management
and fought with destiny,
lived in the fish bowl
and worked in the hosiery mill--
and still ball playered the evenings.

Who robbed and was stabbed,

was put away in Sing-Sing
and put his mother away in Broughton,
who drew the great crowds
and drove them away.

IN ANOTHER COUNTRY

The "paupers cemetery" at
Broughton State Mental Hospital,
I'm looking for a depression-era
ball player's mother's grave.

Most of them are unmarked or marked
by weather-worn granite posts,
washed clean of names or numbers.
Some graves are fixed with metal plaques,

a project that stops in the 20's—
occasionally there's a regular stone;
one declares its occupant was
a "fine artist and musician."

I move slowly over thick trimmed grass,
looking for the right camera angle
through unbearable August heat
and thoughts of Erma Pitts Rudd

who stepped through Sing-Sing's iron gate
with her celebrity convict son
into a New York Times flash so that
the world knew he was her boy

then somehow ended up here
with the demon-haunted and broken,
the utterly forgotten, where shadows
mark a little more earth each day.

ANOTHER NIGHT WHEN I KNOW

that I can stand on my flat dark driveway
and if I look hard across the valley
I will see Tracey Hitchner stepping
off the train at the Hickory station,
holding one suitcase, staring at the
deserted town, ready to head back
to New York on anything leaving,
instead staying, playing outlaw ball,
marrying, working, living sixty years
on the "ugly" Piedmont red dirt,
and I can see big Vince Barton,
arriving half-drunk and late for a game,
showering, just making it to the start,
then slamming five home runs,
a record, illegal as the whole damned league,
and Vince, gone back to Canada and,
for good or bad, never heard from again.
I can see crowds of men in hats and overalls,
women in Sunday dresses, fans sitting
in trees beyond the left field fence,
the hard dirt infield, the cement football
bleachers in right. Looking hard across
the valley, I can see through seventy
years of time, and it's the greatest movie,
the insane miracle of imagination
this drive-in theatre of history.

I AM HAUNTED BY OLD BALL PARKS

I have gone to Lenoir-Rhyne College to stand
out by the brick athletic buildings.
I have turned this way, then that,
trying to see how the base lines ran,
where the wooden slatted fence kept
gray flannel games hidden, how the
grand stand hovered against the tree line.

I have wondered where umpires parked,
to conceal their cars from rabid fans,
how Pud Miller and Norman Small
waited on deck to slam rockets into darkness,
where Stumpy Culbreath stopped his pacing
to tell Vince Barton "Yore in right tonight,"
as if he'd come like Ruth in a black Packard
with a babe on his arm for any other reason.

The grass behind the football stadium
has grown tough through the losing seasons,
haunted as an Indian mound.
It is the grass that grows over graves,
and the ghosts are the wind that blows through it.

JIM POOLE AND THE BASEBALL LIFE

41 in '36, you were still
sticking it in that outlaw league,
.399, 54 rib eyes with half a season to go,
then all those years playing and coaching
the Class D teams:
Mooresville, Statesville, Forest City,
having been there, having felt the hot glow
of the big time, three years in Philly,
then those 50 homers in Nashville,
and too old for another crack.
A college star at sixteen,
born in the tobacco apple foothills,
in the bulls eye of Alexander,
how did you take it,
the year after year scraping by,
waiting for Connie Mack to call again,
for Branch Rickey to ring your bell—
then there were the clinics,
players, umpires, off season cash,
a family to feed through hard times,
and we can only guess who you really were,
what kind of captain,
and what crazy engine
kept you in the game
on first base, on the bench,
that dark faced teen who once
sat with his teammates
under pine trees in 1911,
looking at 64 more years of life,
49 more years of the greatest game.

RAZZ MILLER

A preacher who loved his hounds
so much he ran them Sundays
after church tailing a fox
like the Holy Ghost through fields
into forests, arriving home
for supper and evening prayers.

Once a farm boy himself,
tobacco, cotton, barley—
once a thief on the base paths,
a solid arm in deep right,
a dangerous leadoff man,
a three sport college player.

Lutheran seminary,
then Depression ministry—
switched to teaching, playing
mill ball in the long summers—
and there were those outlaw league
days, the fist fights, the fast play.

Finally a man settled
with school teacher wife, to a
country life of animals
and parishioners: shepherd,
husband, father, hunter, his
own son, taken the "cloth," too.

Retired, Rowan County, NC,
on a summer evening,
after praying with his wife
for the Pope who had been shot,
he went to feed his beloved
hounds; was found dead in their lot.

HAROLD LAIL'S PERMISSION

I stop by to get him to sign
a permission for the new book,
outlaw players, interviews and profiles.

We talk about some players, Pitts, Barton,
Stumpy Culbreath—then he grabs a baseball and
says let me show you how Shaney did it.

Harold presses the ball against his hip, rubs
the edge of his left thumbnail hard into the seams; the
scraping is surprisingly loud.

It takes him thirty seconds, tops.
Then he holds the ball in his big right palm
and says, "Feel the difference now."

I run my fingers along the left seam,
the loose, risen red threads, then the right one,
still packed down in its machine groove.

Harold is smiling. For the first time
I notice he's lost weight since I've seen him,
more like his 1940s mill team pictures.

He tells me about his no-hitter;
he tells me about the bus breaking down
on an overpass in 1938.

He tells me about phonograph needles;
he says last weekend he helped
put siding on a church in West Virginia.

We're out past interviews; when I leave,
I shake his seventy-nine year-old hand,
unable to take on his power with his knowledge.

POEM FOR WINNIE

Late summer storm,
the ambulance horn blows through
the muffled night,
and I am thinking of Winnie Taylor
who sat with us signing books
two months ago, beautiful ninety-one,
stately in her wheelchair,
smiling, hugging minor league fans,
friends, relatives of men
who played with or batted against
Coddle Creek seventy years ago,
Winnie who stayed for four hours,
gave up her wheel chair for a box seat
in the fifth inning and watched
islanders, single A boys disguised
in the throwback uniforms
her husband wore in outlaw days,
Winnie who died three weeks later
in her sleep,
at peace with the baseball gods,
her own words read from our book
at the funeral.
Late summer storm,
the ambulance horn blows through
another magnificent, ghostly night.

82

BROOKFORD

Here is this tan river,
this hundred year old dam,
a huge brick building empty.

Gone are the baggy eyed men,
in grubby overalls and felt hats,
their lint-stuffed lungs,
their yellow cigarette fingers.

Gone are the tubercular women
that doffed and chased children,
their callused hands and hard frowns
darken museum ramparts—
trucks do not come here now
for socks or stockings or yarn.
The old foot bridge has vanished.

The highway blasted the stores;
long ago, the mill houses were
fixed for people and sold.
This town is a fragment,
its great looms gone missing.
The only ghosts left play baseball,
gray willowy shadows in moonlight.

ALABAMA PITTS, WHAT DID YOU LEARN?

What did you learn in Sing Sing?
the open field run, the stiff arm,
how to break the 220 down—
your dark little mother came up
from Georgia to walk through that
iron door with her famous son,
the world for one moment
at your feet, a young TIMES stringer
flashing the image with caught breath
forward nearly seventy glossy years.
Where did you think you were going?
the next Sisler, the next Wagner,
the second coming of the peach—
smoke, all, when the curves began
to drop in Albany, when the game
was coffin tight with best players
every boy wanted to be somehow,
and Dizzy and Paul were re-talking
the language in St. Louis—is that
resolve in your face, or the hardness
of steel bars in gray eyes six years
up the river of missed women and
running catches that stopped
at concertina wire, contracts and
crowds always waiting just
beyond the robbery sentence,
and mother come to get her boy
in her best dress wearing a hat
she could hardly afford. Alabama,
what did you learn in Sing Sing?

84

THE 1912 BROOKFORD MILL BASEBALL TEAM

Under dark trees by a field
in fifteen different poses,
work pants jackets, floppy hats,
fifteen cigarettes still half-
burned ninety-three years later,
meek hounds settled at their feet,
the Brookford Mill baseball team.

When the sun rises through dust,
they will come in their wagon,
haughty-faced, sporting enough
fingers for gloves just barely
bigger than hands, homemade bats,
shotguns against shoulders, yet
no tracked up base path could hide
the rough hunger in those eyes.

THE MIRACLE AT CONCORD

The two mill towns hated each other
And they packed old Webb Field
On a Sunday afternoon in the 20's,
Women dressed in their finest,
Dresses and hats, men in Sunday suits,
Yet there were bottles and knives
And bets aplenty so when the ump
Called a hometown boy out at the plate
In the bottom of the first, they began
To move down from the stands
Toward each other wielding weapons,
And just before the first blows landed,
A rain erupted, biblical in its ferocity,
Four or five inches deep on the field,
And the crowd fled in their ruined finery,
Walking to their lookalike rental houses
Only a few blocks away where
It had not rained a drop.

KIND OF LIKE WOODSTOCK

It was a late August game, 1938,
Hickory and Kannapolis,
Played as the Carolina League
In its third outlaw year
Was about to collapse
In a heap of banned players
And broken owners.
Vince Barton had arrived late
Having driven straight
From a roadhouse bar
In his black Packard
Dragged to the shower
By the batboy and delivered
To Stumpy Culbreath's bench
As the umpire shouted, "Play Ball."
After his fifth home run soared
Into the right field football bleachers,
He shuffled over to the Kannapolis
Side to shake hands with the owner
That had let him go the year before.
The box score for the only nine inning
Game in which a man hit five homers
Declared 600 in attendance,
Probably a boast in this otherwise
Most inconsequential of games.
But to a man, every old guy
I interviewed 70 years hence
Was there with his dad or uncle
Or brother or mother,
Kind of like Woodstock.

THE STORY GOES ON

One after one the old guys
tell me, "We sure did have fun,"
came straight from tailing rip saws,
from stacking cartons of beer,
from teaching high school PE,
from driving a linen truck,
straight to the field changing in
the cabs of Ford pickups or
in the cement block ball field johns,
the clack of cleats across the
dugout slab, a coke, an oatmeal
cake, and the adrenaline to
face a forty-something ex-
minor league pitcher, bent to
prove the eminent gas of
his game—cigarettes between
the machinery of innings.
Nearing or past eighty, their
eyes glisten as we scan through
dog eared photos, players, lean
and hawk-faced in stadiums
preserved by the bright trance of
camera. Their voices
narrate—this kid was from NY,
this guy always lost his glove—
this one made it to the show.
I listen wistfully—they speak excitedly
of memories plowed deep,
now words rising in these fertile rows.

3. HICKORY REBELS

REBELS 1

The Bull set the bench
And talked feverishly to everybody around him,
How to pitch a hitter, where to place the fielders,
When to run, how to place a bet
With the cab driver that ran the game
Out along the left field side.
The Bull had no neck and his uniform
Fit him tightly across his chest and shoulders.
He always kept a ball in his freshly oiled glove
Even though he knew he'd only pinch hit
When it came time to pull the Cuban starter.
As the manager returned from coaching third,
He stopped at the cooler and poured a cup
With the metal dipper and said shut up, Bull
Before he could ask him whatever it was
And the unfazed Bull turned back
To his latest teachable moment.

REBELS 2

The contracts always looked the same:
400-500 month, so the hat passed
By the fans at College Field after a winning start
Or a home run made the difference
In a hard winter as the post-war country
Regained its land legs and the general manager
Who was also an elementary principal
Would meet you in the gray twilight
Behind the school's coal bin
To deliver an extra hundred
From your games' gates,
Yet the real prizes were the girls
That cruised Main Street
Till the line of ballplayers
In front of the town hotel
Diminished to the ones
That were really just there
To pitch pennies or whose fears
Of their wives or girl friends
Back home were greater
Than their current desires.

REBELS 3

He looked through a temple of his fingers
Brushing his chapped lips against the microphone,
And the guttural rendering of his voice
Echoed off the concrete football bleachers
At college field, introductions, advertisements,
Promotions and gimmickry; when he called
For first aid, the groundskeeper delivered
Him a whisky, and at the dimly lit field
He squinted with his one good eye,
And the right one, made of glass
Watched something in another world.

REBELS 4

Maw Sigmon stacked pancakes
And griddled sausage, fried eggs,
And for the northern boys,
Their first taste of buttered grits
At the ten room boarding house,
Two to a bed, midnight curfew,
With Maw waiting like a coach
With a lecture on the porch,
A parent away from home
Following their games,
Dousing their deviltry,
Consoling their lonesomeness.

REBELS 5

The negroes sat the trees beyond left field
and those brave enough stood the fence
behind the right field bleachers
leaning precariously sometimes
on the three strands of barbed wire
till one night one of those nameless fellows
leaned too hard and the wire twisted,
wrapping his pants legs and dangling him backwards
till the city cop that worked the game
came over, already pissed because he'd missed
the Wednesday evening church service,
saw the bloodied old brown work pants,
wild eyes, frantic underwater face,
the busted pint on the ground below,
and announced to no one in particular,
He'll figure out a way down
And walked back in disgust
To the great closed mouth
Of the grand stand gate.

REBELS 6

Alabama Pitts had lost his shine
By 1940 when he signed with Hickory,
And though he batted well
The wolves were never quelled.
He said little, never caroused
With teammates after the games
And he kept a room twenty miles
From his wife and child.
Everybody knew he'd not make it
But women love a bad man
And saw their chance and took it.
When the team released him in August,
He was just a mill hand
Playing mill ball
One step closer to the stabbing
That always awaited.

REBELS 7

Stumpy watched the games in real time,
Time that could raise a cloud of red dust
With the right kind of slide at home plate,
Time that was an outlaw preacher jogging
To center field then racing to stop a left
Center field gapper headed for the football
Field's end zone fence five hundred feet away,
Stumpy watched the games to the rhythm
Of Wrigley gum, 'backer' juice having stained
His teeth and rotted his gums, to the rhythm
Of the pitcher-hitter-catcher's violent dance,
To the rhythm of the crowd's deafening,
Vicious and sometimes mournful roar,
And Stumpy paced beyond the coaching box's
Rectangular limits to splash a dipper
Full of cooler water on his face in real time
And rubbed hound dog ears that could detect
A gun hammer click in another room
Or hear the helicopter spin on a curve ball.

REBELS 8

She wanted to be a batboy like her brother,
Racing in his rubber cleats and white team pants,
To grab the discarded bat as the play wound
To a red dusty stop, but she sat with Daddy
And Uncle Marlan who called Alabama Pitts
A no good jailbird every time he batted.
One day they let her pose with Joe Bear,
The college mascot where games were played,
And she stood there in the yellow dress
She usually wore to church or to parties
With the hardest look she could put on her face
Because she wasn't scared of no bears at all.

REBELS 9

That first bus broke down every trip
So that five cars would carry fourteen
Players and a trunk full of equipment
On what passed for roads north to Lenoir
Or west to Valdese, south to Charlotte
Or Gastonia, east to Statesville, Mooresville,
Or Salisbury where a fan dressed in a
Purple robe called himself the Count of Rowan,
And they drove past the civil war prison camp
Where the game was first played in the South.

REBELS 10

They always made room
For one or two locals,
Mill hands, farm boys
Who got 25 at-bats
Or pitched a couple
August throwaway games,
And they could tell
Their sons and grandsons
They played in the minors
And the stories would grow
Into family legends
Of home runs or
Championship no hitters,
Till sometime after
They're in rest homes,
Befuddled by dementia
Or even passed
When a relative
Anxious to confirm
The family heroics
Checks the online records
And despite the disappointment
Or perhaps out of embarrassment
Tells no one what he finds.

REBELS 11

The old man looked at photos
Of his late wife while he searched
Through a shoe box of dog eared
Pictures for some rare team shots
Of the outlaw Rebels club.
He had huge meaty hands that
Made flipping through the black and
Whites more difficult, yet he
Found them finally, holding
The glossy images up to
His living room lamp so that
I could see Tracey Hitchner
And broad-shouldered Vince Barton
Smiling at either end of
The back row, Stumpy Culbreath
In the middle leaning on
A bat, and the old man smiled
Thinking of bat boy days,
Then looked again at the shot
Of him and his wife, dressed up
Like movie stars, just kids,
Standing in front of their first car,
And he dabbed a Kleenex at
His eye and said, "Sometimes you
Can get lost in this world."

THE BATBOY REMEMBERS REBEL DAYS

He is seventy-seven,
holds five bats across his shoulder,

thirty-six inches, thirty-six ounces;
he stands on the solid balance

of his memory, and when he speaks
about the game, his watery

gray eyes spark to flame, names
called to scratch images to light.

He shows me his stance, his swing,
torso turning on a fifty-year old pitch;

in his front yard, end of a dead end street;
if he remembers them, they will come.

4. EXTRA INNINGS

HICKORY POEMS 1

They had climbed to the top
Of a small mountain and sat
Near the edge overlooking
The southern part of the county
All the way to the lake.
They parked in a gravel drive
That served a small substation
And backpacked six packs
Up the muddy trail.
The sun was low over the lake
And the half dozen ball players
Passed a joint up and down
Till it disappeared in the jaws
Of an alligator clip.
The jokes and laughter
Filled the darkness;
Then the silent melancholy
Claimed them, and they felt
Untouchably independently high
Above their small world,
Yet they sat, left to right,
For reasons they could not explain
In the team batting order.

HICKORY POEMS 2

Dad said to go knock on the trailer door,
So I stood there listening to a woman
Cussing above the sound of a scratchy
Radio playing Charlie Pride or Rich—
I could never keep them straight.
Then the plastic door slapped ajar nearly
Knocking me off the single concrete block
And Frog leaped through the sudden opening
Holding his ball glove over his head
To ward off a broom stick blow from his mom.
Freckle faced with purple kool-aid stained lips,
He dived into the back seat of dad's car.
Why, hello coach, he said, and he settled
In to pick at the scabs on his legs
As Dad drove the gravel road to practice.

HICKORY POEMS 3

The flaming July sun
And the red dust rose
Every time a grounder
Scooted toward the shortstop's glove,
Glancing sometimes off a bit
Of dust red granite into his naked chest
Or off his chin, and he came up
Throwing and spitting blood
From a bitten tongue.
He wore a boy's work pants,
Cut off raggedly above
His bruised ankles
Hiding the electric cord stripes
That daddy put there last night.
He had a broken upper tooth
And the finger he held outside
His glove was jammed and swollen blue.
When it was his turn,
He leaned over the plate
And held the bat cross-handed,
Swinging at every pitch.

WHEN BLAS PITCHED AT BIG RED

Three little league fields built
Like a half pie sliced
In the flood plain of Crane Creek—
When Blas pitched at Big Red,
Parents from the other games
Gathered behind his backstop
To watch his long leg high kick,
His left toe pointed
Toward the sky
As if he were signaling
His alien home world—
Then that straight overarm
His head fallen toward first
And if you listened,
Listened like a baseball man,
You could hear the ball,
Actually hear the ball
Hurtling toward the mitt.

FAITH

Leaving Oklahoma, Mantle,
Corn fed and country handsome,
Listened to his daddy and
After he died young, carried
On conversations with him
In the Yankee centerfield.
Mickey looked up at what stars
He could see, and there was Mutt
Telling him to move in some,
To always hit the cutoff,
But when the game was over,
Mick was all alone with his
Mates, the women, the party,
Walking Manhattan sidewalks,
The latest girlfriend on
His arm, he drunkenly scanned
The empty meaningless sky.

FAITH 2

Mickey Mantle is somewhere
In that deep black winter sky
His serious drunk face, a star,
Loafers and leisure suit smile.
Mickey Mantle is flying over
The farm tonight, circling
The meadow, dashing across
The silhouette of city lights
Like the kid from Commerce
Sprinting to first, the whole
World in his wheels again.

FAITH 3

What about the faith it takes to travel
From Illinois to Rhode Island in 1881
What about the day that you wake
To pitch your 72nd game of the season
Having won 58 bare handed affairs
Your catcher having had a finger amputated
Now returned for the pennant stretch
As the afternoon sun dwindles—
The ball mud black
And you Hoss Radbourn try to raise your arms
Above your splitting headache
Rotator obliterated
Hop stepping in the pitcher's rectangular box
Swinging the arm sideways forward like an
Orangutan
Refusing to wince even as the javelin spasms
Through your shoulder the red headed Ump
Who might have been a Providence cop as well
Calls the perfect strike on the left corner of the
Diamond shaped plate and you can't wait
For the scalding first taste of tavern whisky.

LAST POEMS 112

His childhood was Willie Mays
Scoring all the way from first on a single,
The takeout slide and his cap flying,
A catechism bible left in the rain,
Paul's letters bleeding into the Gospels,
Hacking black snakes with hoe blades,
Hoeing a football field of Irish potatoes,
Smells: the canvas bat bag, chest protector,
Shin guards, dragged through red dirt,
Scuffed dirty baseballs, part of a rulebook.
Library books with taped spines:
Shapiro, Christopher, Nick Adams,
The bookmobile on Mondays,
Like his childhood,
Smoking as it idles.

THE WILLIS HE WAS

He was one of the Willises,
Not the musical ones who played
Long front porches on Sunday afternoons,
Not the bar owners who leased
New pickup trucks for their managers
Because it looked good to roll up thusly
And might afford a powerful getaway
Should circumstances call for such,
I'm talking about the baseball ones,
The three barely literate brothers
Who each bothered for a year of college
Because they knew it was a possible way,
Who lived by the crook in the river
Where they'd found slithers of Spanish gold
Buried in the best potters' clay
Known to exist in the county.
He was the one clocked at 90 mph
When he was sixteen threw inside
Rattle snake strikes till he got
A doctor's daughter cheerleader
Pregnant so that her father
Sent her to an aunt's to stay
And threatened him with statutory
If he ever came around again.
That's the Willis he was,
The one who was never the same.

THE NATURAL

Once he wanted to be a third baseman,
loved the gamble of playing in shallow,
the way a ball could blink up from one hop,
the constant balance it called for, the hands.

He got the scholarship offer, but there
was this girl that lived under his skin,
just sixteen, and he could hardly leave her,
so they went to Gaffney instead, eloped,

moved into a trailer behind her mom's,
and he learned to tail a ripsaw, run a
boring machine, dowel gun, yet sometimes
a new worker would ask him about ball,

and he'd say that school was just not for him.
He'd always had a darkness about him,
a silence that defied conversation,
and soon the wife was pregnant and leaving.

Now he often thought of the hot corner,
lunging to his left for a low line drive,
charging a perfectly placed sacrifice,
awaiting the regret of a foul fly.

SNAPSHOT

What was Murphy thinking in
'46, having sold ads
for the programs all summer,
stopping at each downtown store,
flipping aviators 'round
his right thumb as he promised
to return in a week if
a dry cleaner refused, or the
widow florist asked for credit.

What was Murphy thinking when
he first gripped the microphone,
his white shirt collar lifted,
hair carefully tonic-ed back?
More money, maybe girls
that cruised the players out by
Hotel Hickory, awaiting
the fire-baller Cuban or
that gorgeous Yankee catcher.

At eighteen, maybe just kicks,
a young man, someday mayor,
son of an Irish salesman,
always set for a good time,
would hardly have considered
history, nights to follow,
that it all meant anything
when the cub reporter turned
to snap this precious photo.

CURE

The vocal tics went away when he started to smoke.
In the days before anyone around here knew anything
About Tourette's, he was just nervous,
And even those embarrassing moments
Like when a parent driving scouts to an outing
Turned to the backseat and said, I believe
We have a dove in the car, or in a
7th grade math class when a smart girl
With braces and a Yankee accent
Said, would you please stop it when he couldn't,
Because each soft grunt granted him
A small amount of pleasure or maybe
Held back the flood of whatever in the universe
Was trying to break through
And drown him with too much life,
Though when he took the mound to pitch a game
Or when he set his feet at the plate,
He was calm as the butcher whose
Hands shook till he took up a knife.

WHEN JOHNNY ALLEN WENT INTO THAT BARN

It's gotta be something besides baseball
That gets a man to the end of his rope
At twenty-four, the Class D hookup
Almost certainly over, what they called
A three year player and the three years up.
The last season done, he'd taken
That city boy Dick Stoll back home to hunt.
Tramped through woods and briars
All around his grandpa's foothills farm.
They'd laughed when Dick bout blew
His shoulder from a shotgun kick.
They'd stayed up late and drank moonshine,
Got up early and ate Granny's biscuits,
Sopping in spicy sausage gravy.
And that Yankee boy told stories
About back home Ohio
Almost good as Grandpa
While the woodstove crackled
A piece of green pine
And Johnny stobbed an oily rag
Through a shotgun barrel
And looked down it like he would
In a couple months
One last time.

JOHN BILLY'S MUGGING

When the boy just turned ten,
Herschel got him a ticket
The day all the schools let out
For the big league train to stop
For the exhibition game.
The crowd at college ball field
Spilled forth from the stands right up
To the foul lines where he sat
Legs crossed between two women
He'd seen at the Sunday church.
The sun shone across his face
And it was better than his
Best barber shop shoe shining
Day; he watched Bob Feller throw
His practice pitches and heard
The thwack of the leather mitt.
When the first foul ball bounced past
First base, John Billy was set,
Snagging it with his left hand
And he held it up in the light,
The first baseball of his own
Till a grown man cuffed his ears
From behind, so hard that he
Dropped the ball and the man scooped
It into his pocket and
Melted back into the throng.

116

SCRAPDOG, 1944

Kids just went where they wanted then;
There wasn't a rec center or little league,
But the mill hill boys had a team,
The town school boys had their teams,
And we'd walk two or three miles
To a school playground or a vacant lot
Big enough to put out rocks for bases,
And maybe somebody's older brother
Would umpire from behind the pitcher,
And the ball would be one stolen
From outside the college field
By a boy who had his ass beat
On the first try but somehow escaped.
Three or four guys had gloves that
We shared with the other team
So that everybody but the outfielders
Had one, and the catcher might be
Beaten to a pulp or busted in the nuts,
But the game went on till the first
Team scored twenty runs and then
A fight usually commenced
Till we got so tired of cussing and punching
That we limped back to the hill
Full of victory and the anticipation
Of the next Saturday and the next
Till the day we'd have to go to high school
With those town boys and we'd
Be fighting them again
For their girlfriends.

SOMEONE ELSE'S BOY

Sunlight sewn across the field
Like millions of perfect teeth
You could not settle to watch
The one who never fit in
And you knew that God made him
That God distributed burdens
To those who could handle them
And you heard his mother pray
When it came his time to hit
He stood there confused leaning
Bat on his shoulder watching
A strike then a ball then a
Strike as your stomach tightened
And you hoped with all you had
Uttering your own quick prayer
But he swung late like the gate
That closes after the cows
Are all gone and his mother
Felt angry then bitter and
She turned away as if he
Were someone else's boy.

CASEY'S LAST AT-BAT

You live beyond the disturbing strikeouts,
beyond the boozy characters you are made of,
beyond the brawn you once became.

One day the sky is sincerely blue
and the field is excitingly green.
It is your temple familiar.

And you make your way
from the circle of preparation
to the rectangle of decision, one last time.

In a world set to sneak into a spotless century,
you dig in and wait
for eternity.

JERICHO ROBINSON

Came out the wrong barrel
Held the bat cross handed
Fielded the ball with his left hand
Then took the glove off to throw
Rifle shots from right to third
Dad worked and worked
To change his stance his hands
Found him an old glove
At the bottom of the bat bag
Worked and worked like
He was training a boxer
But Jericho snapped back wrong
After dad turned his shoulder
Or moved his head a bit.

I rode the back seat with Jericho
He sat there looking ahead
Never said a word till one night
When dad had stopped
To get us burgers and cokes
He looked over at me said
Wintertime at my house
It so cold the mice wear ear muffs
Then he looked back ahead
At the seat in front of him and
At the crazy moonlight
Gusting through the windshield.

THE IMMORTALS
For Dick Stoll

A little guy from Ohio,
Who pitched fine but briefly,
Then married better and stayed,
The way they often did
Just after the war
When the parks refilled
With fans and hope and pride,
Winning on every side,
So that if you played it right
And remembered it well,
Your story and theirs;
When the time arrived to tell.
You became immortal.

THE SIGNING OF HOYT WILHELM

When Hoyt Wilhelm brought
His butterflies to Hickory,
Nobody had ever heard of him;
At the meeting in Hill's Café
Hubbell said "he's got
No curve ball, and he's
Surely got no fastball;
All he's got is that knuckle ball,"
But Sammy Bell, Duke grad
And Hickory manager
Who'd not only played
For the great Jack Coombs
But had also tried to hit
The Iredell farm boy's
Knuckle ball said, "Carl,"
Not Mr. Hubbell as
The Giants' chain of command
And surely his historical
Imminence might demand, but
He said, "Carl," in his Carolina drawl;
"It's all he needs."

BASEBALL APOSTATE

IT was the most brutal form of rebellion,
Denying the old man, after thousands
Of hours spent as a side yard battery
As the boy grew taller and stronger
And the pitches more dangerous,
Sometimes intentionally so
That the old man's shins purpled
And he even considered giving it up,
Paying the high school catcher
From down the street to sit on
His bean pickin chair, but the Lord
Had told him to teach his son to pitch
And he always listened to the Lord
Even when the Lord asked for crazy things.
The afternoon the boy told him on the ride home
From school, the old man couldn't talk
At first, and the boy knew that his pitches
Could only hurt if he refused to throw them.

HOW YOU GET TO HEAVEN

My dad's magical thinking
Transported him beyond reality.
He believed his sons would
Be major leaguers, and that
Having not worked out,
He believed his grandsons
Would be major leaguers;
Then he eventually believed
That he might just have been
A major leaguer at some point,
About the same time he became
Convinced that someone
Had moved him to the wrong house
During the middle of the night
And had carefully placed
All his furniture where it was
When we sat and talked about it,
And he also believed when
He called me at three in the morning
That if I left my house immediately
And came over to his to transpose
His life story that his chances
Of being elected to the hall of fame
In honor of his major league
Pitching career might be improved
So I drove forthwith and arrived
With an ink pen and notebook,
After which I sat and he began,
I was born on a dirt farm
Next to a muddy creek
In rural Rowan County
And I wrote it down
As outside I could hear
The roar of the crickets
And inside I could hear
The buzz of the fluorescent light.

124

CARRYING ONE WHO'D CARRIED US

Snow banked the icy graveyard path
Where we carried his red oak casket,
So heavy that we slipped but held on,
As if the box contained as well as him
All the home runs and strikeouts,
Rare triples and overrun bases,
The wave of the crowd roar
That once transported him from
The shore of one season to the next.

THE FOURTH SON

He was eleven years old, seventy pounds,
But he had a rocket arm,
And he could catch every pitch without signals
From a six foot Goliath
Whose minor league pitcher daddy
Had taught him to throw curve balls,
Screw balls, knuckle balls,
Overhand, or side arm.
He was eleven years old,
His working class parents too
Busy to come to the games,
So my dad fathered him
Like he were his fourth son;
Yet many years later,
When Tim died of cancer,
Dad could not go to the funeral
Even though he had been to hundreds,
Having preached the most of them,
Always finding the strength
To say the last words over the dead,
Though he could not find them
For one of his own.

A FATHER TELLS HIS SON

There will always be those
Who think they can strike you out,
But you don't have to crowd the plate
Or choke up because they exist.

CONVICTION

He taught me to believe
Beyond my senses, beyond
My limited ability.
He held his mitt knee high
On the outside corner
Willing the ball to arrive
With a gentle pop,
Held the mitt
As if he'd not move it
Though the mad pitch
Might veer toward his face,
And I threw without thinking
About arm angle
Or release point,
Without aiming or
Shifting my shoulder.
I threw that ball
With emotionless belief
And he caught it
The same way.

THE WAY IT ALL ENDS

Let it be like the old days:
a close call at the plate,
a fight in the grandstand
between men in work clothes
and Clark Kent hats,
a forfeit after the road team
refuses to take the field in the eighth,
the umpires sprinting
toward the left field gate,
as the PA announcer tries
to think of something to say.

Let there be rocks thrown
at the escaping bus,
fans from both sides
calling for a God to smite
their mortal enemies,
let it be 1938 with a war
about to suck these folks
across oceans into foxholes,
to save this hardscrabble world.
If it all must end, let the old curses
soar through the black night forever.

CPSIA information can be obtained at www.ICGtesting.com
Printed in the USA
LVOW10s1531041016

507374LV00016B/1516/P

9 780692 719701